USBORNE

STARS AND PLANETS

Alastair Smith
Designed by Jane Rigby and Karen Webb
Consultant: Stuart Atkinson

Contents

OUR SOLAR SYSTEM

The Solar System is made up of the Sun and all the objects that spin around it.

The Sun

The Sun is a star – that is, a massive ball of exploding gases. It applies a pulling force, called gravity, to everything nearby. This keeps objects in their places, going around and around the Sun.

The planets

The largest things that spin around the Sun are the planets. The Earth is one of the planets. Scientists have discovered nine planets so far.

Asteroid Belt

Mars

Venus

Mercury

Earth

Sun

Great and small

The biggest planet in the Solar System is Jupiter, followed by Saturn. The smallest planet is Pluto.

Pluto

Neptune

Uranus

Saturn

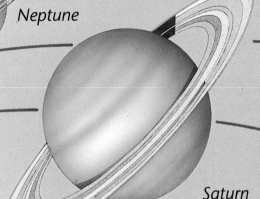

Jupiter

Asteroids

Asteroids are large chunks of rock, or rock and metal. They are dotted all over the Solar System. However, most of them lie between Jupiter and Mars in a band called the Asteroid Belt.

Moons

Many planets have moons going around them. The Earth has only one moon, but some planets have more. For example, Saturn has at least 18 moons.

Most moons are balls of rock and ice. Many have craters, mountains and valleys. One of Jupiter's moons may even have an ocean.

THE SUN

The Sun is so big that you could fit the Earth inside it more than a million times. Compared with some other stars, though, the Sun is tiny.

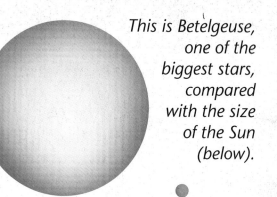

This is Betelgeuse, one of the biggest stars, compared with the size of the Sun (below).

Exploding gas

Like all stars, the Sun is a massive ball of exploding gases. It gives off huge amounts of heat and light. This is sunshine. Without it, life could not exist on Earth.

Sunspots

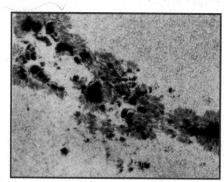

The Sun's surface is often marked with dark areas, called sunspots. These areas are slightly cooler than their surroundings.

The bubbling surface of the Sun

Solar flares

Solar flares are huge explosions which often occur above sunspots. They blast huge amounts of energy out into space.

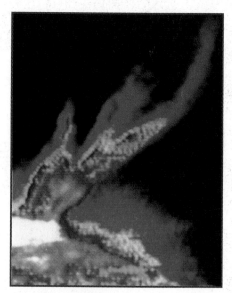

A solar flare

WARNING! Never look directly at the Sun. Its rays will hurt your eyes. They may even blind you.

THE MOON

The Moon spins around and around the Earth. It is about four times smaller than our planet.

The surface

The Moon's surface is covered with deep craters and high mountains. Many of the craters were made by giant objects that hit the Moon.

A city the size of London, England could fit inside the biggest crater.

People have been to the Moon. They collected samples of rock and soil.

Eratosthenes, one of the Moon's craters

One of the first men on the Moon

THE ROCKY PLANETS

Five planets in our Solar System have hard rocky surfaces. They are Mercury, Venus, Earth, Mars and Pluto.

Earth

Venus

Venus is covered with a blanket of gas. Its clouds can rain acid, which would destroy any living thing that was on its surface.

Venus

Mercury

Mercury is the closest planet to the Sun. During the day it gets four times hotter than boiling water!

The photograph below, showing Mercury's surface, was taken by Mariner 10.

Mariner 10 space probe

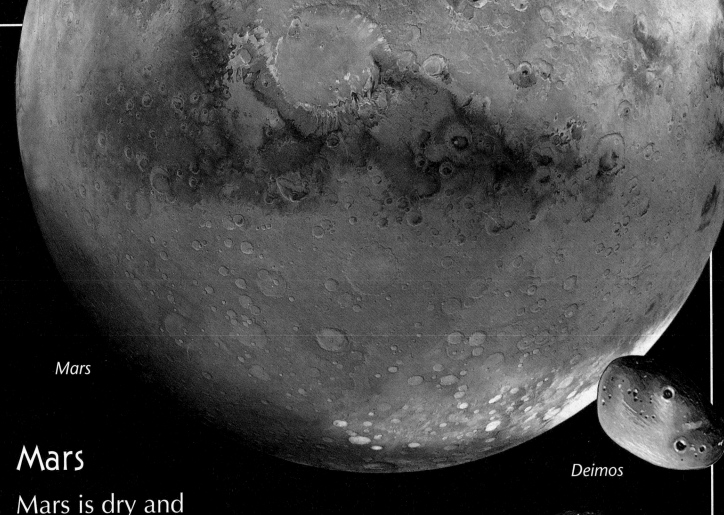

Mars

Mars

Mars is dry and dusty. Its surface looks red and rusty. Huge storms rage for weeks, blasting dust all over its surface.

Mars has two moons – Deimos and Phobos. Both are smaller than the moon which goes around the Earth.

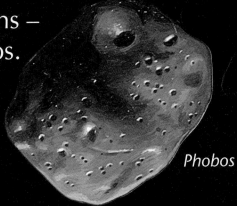

Deimos

Phobos

Pluto

Pluto is the tiniest planet of all. Most of the time, it is the farthest planet from the Sun.

Pluto's moon is called Charon. Compared to the size of Pluto it is fairly big.

Pluto and Charon

PLANET EARTH

Earth is the only place in the whole of space where living things have been found so far.

The Moon goes around and around the Earth.

Layers

The Earth is made up of layers, as shown below. Mercury, Venus and Mars have similar layers.

The crust. Mostly made of rock.

Mantle. Hot rock, some of it is liquid.

Outer core. Made of hot swirling liquid.

Inner core. Made mostly of solid iron.

Water and air

The Earth's distance from the Sun gives it just the right temperature for water to exist as a liquid.

In fact, most of the Earth is covered by water. It forms the planet's vast seas and oceans.

This picture of the Earth was taken by a space satellite.

Earth also has breathable air around it. Animals and plants need breathable air as well as water in order to live.

Wind from the Sun

The Sun blows a nonstop wind out into space. The wind gets trapped above Earth's north and south poles. It causes beautiful light displays, called auroras.

An aurora

GAS GIANTS

The four biggest planets – Jupiter, Saturn, Uranus and Neptune – are known as the gas giants. They are all gigantic balls of gas with rock in the middle.

Europa

Three of Jupiter's moons

Callisto

Io

Jupiter

Jupiter is the biggest planet in the Solar System. It has 16 moons going around it. Several space probes have been sent to explore Jupiter.

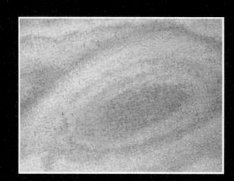

This huge mark on Jupiter is the Great Red Spot. It is an endless raging storm.

The Galileo space probe took pictures of Jupiter.

Jupiter

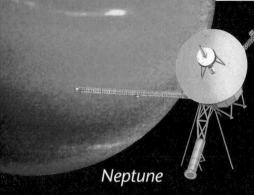
Neptune

The Voyager 2 space probe visited Neptune in 1989.

Uranus – as seen by the Hubble Space Telescope

Neptune

Neptune has a cloud, called the Scooter, which races around the planet in just 16 hours.

Uranus

Uranus rolls on its side like a ball. The other planets spin like tops as they travel around the Sun.

Below are four of Saturn's 18 moons.

Mimas

Enceladus

Tethys

Saturn

Saturn

Saturn has beautiful rings around it. They are made up of rocks and dust.

Titan

HEAVENLY BODIES

Space is mostly made up of nothing but empty gaps. But it also contains things such as asteroids and comets. Far, far away there are millions of stars.

Asteroids

Asteroids are large chunks of rock, or rock and metal. They float around like giant pieces of space litter.

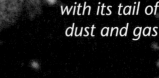

A comet, with its tail of dust and gas

Comets

Comets are giant blocks of ice and rock. They speed through space like dirty snowballs. As they get close to the Sun, they start melting, giving off giant tails of gas and dust.

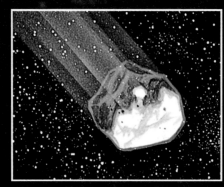

Comet flying through space

Gaspra, one of the largest asteroids

Stars

Stars are enormous, but they are so far away from us that they just sparkle like jewels in the night sky.

Stars gather in huge collections called galaxies. The Sun lies in a galaxy called the Milky Way Galaxy.

It would take thousands of years for a space probe from Earth to reach even the nearest star.

A galaxy

EXPLORING SPACE

Scientists have been sending rockets up into space for over 40 years. They still use them to launch space probes to explore the Solar System – and beyond.

Moon missions

About 30 years ago, people went to the Moon for the first time. Back on Earth you could watch on TV as astronauts explored the Moon's dusty surface.

The first steps on the Moon

Space stations

Space stations are laboratories that float in space. Scientists may stay on them for several months. The most famous of all is Mir, a Russian station launched in 1986.

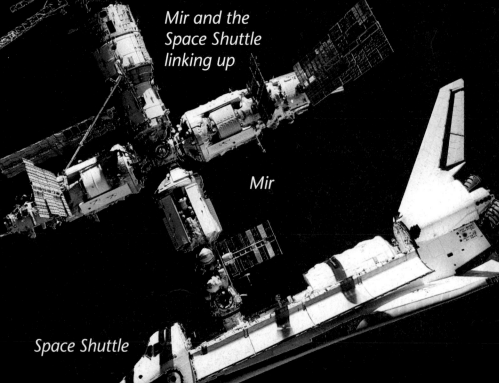

Mir and the Space Shuttle linking up

Mir

Space Shuttle

The USA's Space Shuttle blasts off on a new mission every few months, carrying scientists and equipment up into space.

Space Shuttle

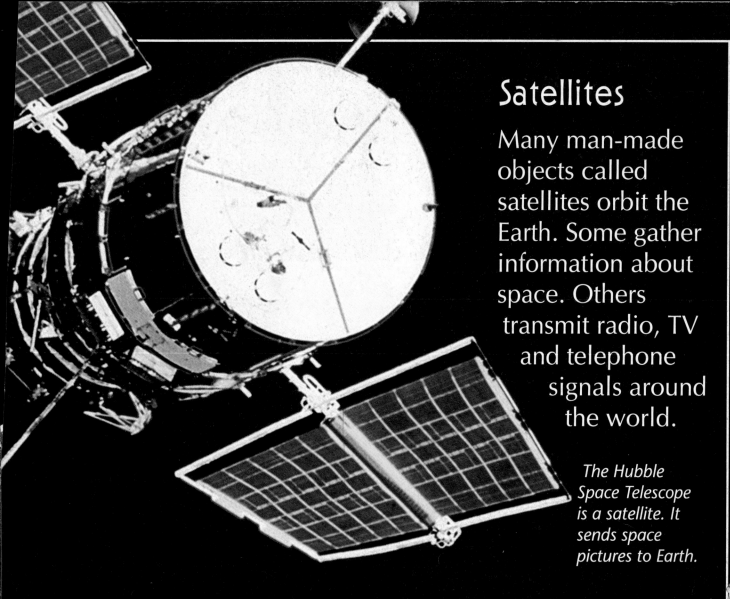

Satellites

Many man-made objects called satellites orbit the Earth. Some gather information about space. Others transmit radio, TV and telephone signals around the world.

The Hubble Space Telescope is a satellite. It sends space pictures to Earth.

Space probes

Space probes travel great distances to explore the Solar System. They carry no people and are controlled by scientists on Earth.

This space probe has landed on Mars.

Space probes can take years to reach their target, because they have to cover such huge distances.

A space probe

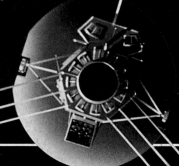

INDEX

Acknowledgements

Additional editorial by Kirsteen Rogers. Computer artwork by Fiona Johnson.

Photo credits key: top – t; middle – m; bottom – b; left – l; right – r.
© Digital Vision (Cover; 4 tr, mr, b; 5 t, m, b; 6 tl; 7 t; 8 t; 8-9; 9 t; 10 m, b; 10-11 t, m; 12 t; 13 t; 14 t, b; 15 t, b).
NASA (4 tl, m; 6 tr, m, b; 11 r; 15 m).

Every effort has been made to trace and acknowledge ownership of copyright. The publishers will be glad to make suitable arrangements with any copyright holder whom it has not been possible to contact.